# Look at the shoots!

Written by Clare Helen Welsh
Photographed by Will Amlot

**Collins**

# Look at the lab!

# We need to set things up.

# 1 Cut off the roots.

## 2 Fill the jars at the tap.

## 3 Pick a jar, then mix.

## 5 Now we wait.

Look at the shoots!

9

# The shoots are red!

# Will the bud turn red too?

# It is the shoots!

# In the lab

# After reading

**Letters and Sounds:** Phase 3

**Word count:** 54

**Focus phonemes:** /ai/ /ee/ /oo/ /oo/ /ar/ /ow/ /ur/

**Common exception words:** the, put, we, to, are

**Curriculum links:** Understanding the World: The World

**Early learning goals:** Reading: use phonic knowledge to decode regular words and read them aloud accurately; demonstrate understanding when talking with others about what they have read

## Developing fluency

- Practise reading out the speech bubble with your child using expression.
- Encourage your child to sound talk and then blend the words, e.g. r/oo/t/s **roots**. It may help to point to each sound as your child reads.
- Then ask your child to reread the sentence to support fluency and understanding.

## Phonic practice

- Look through the book. How many words can your child find with the /ow/ sound? (*now, wow*)
- Can your child think of any words that rhyme with the word **now**? These words have the /ow/ sound at the end. (e.g. *now, how, wow, cow*)

## Extending vocabulary

- Ask your child:
  - **Roots** are part of a plant. Do you know any other parts of the plant? (e.g. *leaves, stem, shoots, bud, flower*)
  - A **jar** is a type of container. Can you think of any other types of containers? (e.g. *jug, beaker, pot, pan, watering can*)